Cornerstones of Freedom

The War of 1812

ANDREW SANTELLA

CHILDREN'S PRESS®
A Division of Grolier Publishing
New York • London • Hong Kong • Sydney
Danbury, Connecticut

Reading Consultant: Linda Cornwell, Coordinator of School Quality and
Professional Improvement, Indiana State Teachers Association

Visit Children's Press on the Internet at:
http://publishing.grolier.com

Library of Congress Cataloging-in-Publication Data

Santella, Andrew.
    The War of 1812 / Andrew Santella.
      p. cm.—(Cornerstones of freedom)
    Includes index.
    Summary: Discusses the causes, events, and aftermath of the
War of 1812.
    ISBN 0-516-21597-3 (lib bdg.)   0-516-27281-0 (pbk.)
    1. United States—History—War of 1812—Juvenile literature.
[1. United States—History—War of 1812.] I. Title. II. Series.
E354 .S26 2001
973.5'2—dc21
00-023534
                                                    99-14957
                                                       CIP

GROLIER
PUBLISHING

Bound for the Mediterranean Sea, the United States warship *Chesapeake* set sail from Virginia on June 22, 1807. Although the sailors on the *Chesapeake* didn't know it, they were in danger. British ships in the area had been ordered to stop them.

British officers believed that some British deserters had joined the crew of the *Chesapeake*. The officers wanted to stop and search the ship and arrest any British deserters. When the *Chesapeake* passed some British ships, just a few miles from shore, one of them—the *Leopard*—chased down the *Chesapeake*.

The commander of the *Leopard* pulled his ship close to the *Chesapeake* and asked U.S. Commodore James Barron if he had any British deserters on board. Barron said he did not know of any—but that answer didn't satisfy the commander of the *Leopard*. He demanded to search the *Chesapeake*. When permission was denied, he opened fire on the U.S. ship. Four American sailors were killed, and eighteen others were wounded.

Sailors from the Leopard *prepare to board the* Chesapeake *to search for deserters.*

The British finally boarded the ship and arrested the sailors they said were British deserters, and then executed them. All but one of the sailors turned out to be Americans.

Americans were outraged by what had happened to the innocent men on the *Chesapeake*. The *Washington Federalist* reported that "All cried aloud for . . . [revenge]." President Thomas Jefferson ordered the British to make reparations, or repay the United States, for their action.

The death of the sailors on board the *Chesapeake* was the most dramatic example of the tense relationship between Great Britain and the United States since the Revolutionary War ended in 1783. The two nations still disagreed on a number of issues. British ships sometimes stopped U.S. ships and impressed seamen, or forced them into service in the British Royal Navy. The British claimed they only took British seamen, but some six thousand U.S. men were forced into the British navy between 1803 and 1812. They had to take orders from British officers, work on British ships, and even fight in Britain's European wars.

Throughout the early 1800s, Great Britain and France were fighting for control of Europe. The impact of their battles was felt even in the United States. The newly independent nation

Thousands of Americans were forced into service in the British Royal Navy before the War of 1812.

In 1812, France had control of most of Europe.

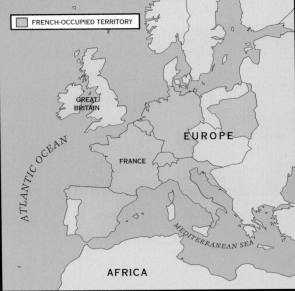

FRENCH-OCCUPIED TERRITORY

GREAT BRITAIN

ATLANTIC OCEAN

EUROPE

FRANCE

MEDITERRANEAN SEA

AFRICA

wanted to remain neutral—not taking sides. However, both Britain and France put restrictions, or limitations, on U.S. trade. The limits on trade strangled American commerce. To make matters worse, British and French ships seized nearly one thousand U.S. ships between 1807 and 1812.

Congress struck back by passing the Embargo Act in December 1807. In part, this law banned all exports—goods sent to another country for trade or sale. The idea was to punish Britain and France, but the plan backfired. The United States exported $108 million worth of goods in 1807 but just $22 million the following year. American businesses suffered, and many workers lost their jobs.

The United States and Great Britain tried to reach an agreement. Great Britain offered the United States reparations for the *Chesapeake* affair. There were so many other problems between the two nations that a final settlement was not reached for four years. By 1811, Great Britain and the United States were on the brink of war.

Henry Clay

Congress was growing more and more furious with Great Britain. Some younger members of Congress from southern and western states wanted to take action against Britain. This group became known as the War Hawks. They were led by Henry Clay of Kentucky. Although Clay was only thirty-four years old and had never served in Congress before, he was elected Speaker of the House of Representatives, a very powerful position. Clay worked hard behind the scenes to shape the government's goals and plans.

Clay and the other War Hawks believed Great Britain was trying to crush U.S. commerce with its restrictions on trade. They were also angry that Britain was slow to settle American complaints about impressing seamen.

When war with American Indians who lived near the Great Lakes broke out, it further complicated U.S.–British relations. The Indians were led by two Shawnee warriors, Tecumseh and his brother, Tenskwatawa. They wanted to stop settlers from taking over their land, but most Americans were sure that British officials in Canada had urged the Indians to go to war.

This statue of Tecumseh is at the United States Naval Academy in Annapolis, Maryland.

In the fall of 1811, U.S. forces under William Henry Harrison defeated Tenskwatawa and his troops in the Battle of Tippecanoe, at what is now Battle Ground, Indiana. However, many people believed that as long as the British controlled Canada, American settlers on the frontier would never be safe from attack.

On November 5, 1811, President James Madison told Congress that Britain had "waged war on our lawful commerce." He urged Congress to prepare the nation for war. Congress, led by the War Hawks, went into action. It expanded the U.S. Army. It set aside money to buy ammunition and build coastal fortifications. Warships were readied for battle.

Even as the U.S. Congress was preparing for war, Great Britain was trying to keep peace. The British Royal Navy began treating U.S. ships and sailors with more respect. To avoid clashes, British ships stayed out of U.S. waters. Britain and the United States even reached a settlement on the *Chesapeake–Leopard* affair. England's foreign secretary, Lord Castlereagh, finally removed the restrictions on American trade on June 16, 1812.

By then it was too late. News of Lord Castlereagh's announcement took weeks to reach the United States. In the meantime, President Madison and Congress were moving toward a declaration of war. On June 1, Madison sent Congress a secret message accusing Britain of urging American Indians in the Great Lakes region to go to war. However, most of Madison's message was about British violations at sea.

Madison said that Britain had impressed U.S. sailors, violated U.S. waters, and set up illegal blockades. He suggested that Britain was continuing to treat the United States like a colony.

Madison did not declare war himself. Only Congress could do that, but many people in Congress believed that a second war with Britain was needed to secure U.S. independence once and for all. They thought the nation should go to war to defend "free trade and sailors' rights." One of the War Hawks—John C. Calhoun of South Carolina—introduced a bill declaring war in the House of Representatives. After just two days of discussion, it was passed by a vote of 79–49.

Action in the Senate took longer. Arguments went on for two weeks. It wasn't until June 17, 1812, that the Senate approved the war declaration by a vote of 19–13. The next day, President Madison signed the bill into law. The War of 1812 had begun.

The war could easily have been avoided. The United States declared war two days after Britain had removed its restrictions on U.S. trade. If members of Congress had known about the British action, they might have changed their minds about the need for war. Even so, the vote to declare war was very close. In fact, it was the closest vote on a declaration of war in U.S. history.

The United States was not well prepared for war. Soldiers often deserted. The state militia lacked training and proper equipment. The government had trouble supplying, feeding, and paying the troops. These problems caused the war to start badly for the Americans.

President Madison and General Henry Dearborn developed a plan for a three-pronged assault on the British in Canada. The United States would attack near Niagara Falls, New York, near Detroit, Michigan, and along the northern shore of Lake Champlain. Very little went as planned. In August, U.S. General William Hull surrendered his troops at Fort Detroit to the British. At about the same time, Potawatomi Indians massacred troops fleeing Fort Dearborn in Chicago.

Fort Dearborn guarded the mouth of the Chicago River, an important waterway.

In October, an American invasion attempt was turned back at Queenston Heights, near Niagara Falls. Nearly one thousand U.S. troops were trapped and forced to surrender. In January 1813, another American force was defeated at Frenchtown, in present-day Monroe, Michigan.

The third major campaign, along Lake Champlain, was called off before it ever started. The U.S. land invasion of Canada failed on all three fronts. To make matters even worse, the British had gained control of large portions of the Northwest Territory—present-day Illinois, Indiana, Ohio, Wisconsin, Minnesota, and Michigan. One newspaper wrote that the campaign had brought nothing but "disaster, defeat, disgrace, and ruin and death."

1 Lake Champlain
2 Baltimore
3 Niagara Falls
4 York (Toronto)
5 Detroit
6 Chicago
7 New Orleans

During the War of 1812, most major land battles took place near water.

Some Americans believed that the nation should not have been fighting the war at all. People in New England were strongly against the war because it was hurting their businesses. The governors of Massachusetts and Connecticut refused to send soldiers to battle and provide supplies to the federal government. Connecticut's General Assembly condemned the war.

About the only thing that went right for the United States in 1812 was the war at sea. The small U.S. Navy performed surprisingly well against the mighty British Royal Navy. British ships had ruled the seas for more than a century. The size of the British navy was staggering. It had more than a thousand ships, but in 1812, they were scattered all around the globe. Some were involved in Britain's war with France. Many were not available for action against the United States.

The first major victory of the war for the United States came at sea. On August 19, the USS *Constitution* spotted the British ship HMS *Guerriere* about 750 miles (1,207 kilometers) east of Boston. The *Constitution* was considered the best frigate in the U.S. Navy, and its battle with *Guerriere* showed why. First, Captain Isaac Hull outsmarted his British counterpart, James R. Dacres. Hull ordered the *Constitution* into a position where

The USS Constitution, *or "Old Ironsides," was built in Boston and launched in 1797. To celebrate the frigate's two-hundredth anniversary, the ship sailed the waters of Massachusetts Bay in 1997.*

it could do the most damage to the British ship. Then the *Constitution* poured on the firepower. Its forty-four guns blasted the hull of the thirty-eight-gun *Guerriere* and destroyed its masts. Dacres had no choice but to surrender. Meanwhile, the *Constitution* was surviving British cannon fire well. One sailor on board saw a British shot bounce off the side of the ship and declared, "Her sides are made of iron!" From then on, the ship was known as "Old Ironsides."

On October 15, the frigate USS *United States* defeated HMS *Macedonian* near the Madeira Islands, off the northwest coast of Africa. After Captain Stephen Decatur forced the British ship to surrender, his crew took over the *Macedonian* and sailed it back to Newport, Rhode Island. It was the only time a British ship was ever brought back to a U.S. port as a prize of war. The *Constitution* won another sea battle in December, when it fought HMS *Java* off the coast of Brazil. The *Java* was so badly damaged that it had to be sunk.

Although the U.S. Navy lost three of its own ships, it defeated seven British ships in 1812. The navy's success boosted American spirits. The victories at sea helped make up for the failures on land. The conquest of Canada, which many had expected to be easy, turned out to be a disaster. However, the war at sea, where Britain seemed to have a huge advantage, was being won by the United States. Americans were delighted at embarrassing the British Royal Navy. "The bully has been disgraced by an infant," said one congressman.

By 1813, the United States was more prepared for war. Outstanding generals, such as Andrew Jackson and William Henry Harrison, took command of the troops. An increase in pay resulted in more and better volunteers. The United States had twice as many troops in 1813 as it had in 1812.

Andrew Jackson (left) and William Henry Harrison (right) won victories during the War of 1812 that made them famous. Each man eventually became president of the United States.

Still determined to invade Canada, the United States hoped to take control of the waters of the Great Lakes—an important goal to both sides. The region surrounding the lakes was densely wooded and lacked good roads, making it very difficult to move large forces and their supplies by land. The lakes, however, could serve as a water highway. Whoever controlled the lakes would also have an advantage on land.

The British Royal Navy controlled the lakes in the first year of the war. The United States set out to change that. In April 1813, Captain Isaac Chauncey and General Zebulon Pike launched an attack from Lake Ontario on York, present-day Toronto. Pike's army drove the British from York and took over. They burned down government buildings and stole valuable goods. Later in the war, the British would take their revenge.

Zebulon Pike

Commodore Oliver H. Perry points toward the Niagara *during the Battle of Lake Erie.*

Meanwhile, on Lake Erie, Commodore Oliver H. Perry was putting together a U.S. fleet, or a group of ships. He began building four new warships and bought four more. Finally, he added a British ship that had been captured a few months earlier.

In September 1813, Perry sailed out to meet the British fleet. The battle that followed was so intense that Perry had to call on wounded men to pitch in. When his ship was disabled, Perry and a few crew members jumped into a smaller boat and rowed to another American ship, the *Niagara*. Then Perry sailed the *Niagara* back into the British fleet and continued the fight. Within a few hours, the largest British ships were destroyed, and their commanders were killed or wounded. The entire British fleet on Lake Erie surrendered. "We have met the enemy and they are ours," Perry wrote after the battle. His victory gave the United States an edge in the Great Lakes region.

*We have met the enemy and they are ours:
Two Ships, two Brigs one Schooner & one Sloop.
Yours, with great respect and esteem
O H Perry.*

Perry proudly proclaims victory in his report to General William Henry Harrison.

The British tried to invade Ohio in May 1813, and again in July, but they were turned back both times. With Perry in control of Lake Erie, the British troops were unable to get supplies by water, so they retreated into Canada with their American Indian allies. The U.S. troops quickly took Detroit back, and then they chased the British. Forces under William Henry Harrison caught up with the British at Moraviantown, about 50 miles (80.5 km) east of Detroit. The British formed defensive lines. An American force on horseback charged and cut through the lines, catching the British in a cross fire. On October 5, 1813, the great American Indian leader Tecumseh was killed near Thamesville, Canada, and the British force surrendered. The Battle of the Thames, as it was called, gave the United States control of the Northwest Territory. American Indian tribes that had been on Great Britain's side then began to side with the United States.

Another problem with American Indians erupted along the Georgia border. There, a group of Creek Indians began attacking settlements in the summer of 1813. Called Red Sticks, the Creeks were partly inspired by the example of Tecumseh. They attacked Fort Mims, in present day Alabama, killing nearly 250 people. Andrew Jackson, a major general in the Tennessee militia, organized a force of 2,500 to fight the Creeks. His forces defeated two groups of Creeks in the fall of 1813. The following spring, he trapped a force of about one thousand Creeks at Horseshoe Bend, Alabama, and won a decisive victory. Jackson forced the Creek leaders to sign the Treaty of Fort Jackson. As a result, the Creeks lost more than half their land.

Jackson, Harrison, and Perry gave the United States important victories in the Northwest and the South. Along the Niagara and St. Lawrence Rivers, the story was different. The British destroyed towns in upstate New York. "The whole frontier from Lake Ontario to Lake Erie is . . . destroyed," wrote the governor of New York. Another invasion of Canada stalled when British ships won control of Lake Champlain, on the border between New York and Vermont.

The British navy also blockaded the U.S. coast, seriously hurting American trade. The blockade also kept American warships trapped in port.

They fought only four naval battles on the high seas in 1813, and they lost three of them.

The worst news for the United States came from Europe. There, Great Britain and her allies were defeating France. This meant that Britain would soon be able to send more troops and supplies to North America for the war with the United States. The United States had won some important victories in 1813, but it had been unable to deliver a knockout blow. Now the United States would face the full military force of Great Britain.

At the Battle of Fort Niagara in 1813, an American soldier's wife named Betsy Doyle is said to have helped fight the British.

The British sent about fourteen thousand new troops to North America. They began attacking the U.S. forces. In 1814, the British launched invasions along the Canadian border, in Chesapeake Bay, and in the Gulf of Mexico.

On the Canadian border, U.S. forces fought bravely. In July 1814, they defeated the British at the Battle of Chippewa, and they held their own against Britain's best in the Battle of Lundy's Lane. Elsewhere, the British were

Dolley Madison

advancing into U.S. territory. They occupied several towns along the coast of Maine, and they used their naval power to establish bases in Chesapeake Bay, not far from Washington, D.C.

In August 1814, the British sent twenty warships and boatloads of experienced troops to Chesapeake Bay. They landed in Maryland and headed for Washington, D.C. The Americans were slow to organize defenses for the nation's capital. So when the British swept aside a U.S. force on the outskirts of Washington, the capital was left defenseless. President Madison, Attorney General Richard Rush, and Secretary of State James Monroe fled to Virginia. Madison's wife, Dolley, took charge of removing government records, but she had to leave her own possessions behind. When the British marched into Washington on August 24, several officers

made their way to the White House. "We found a supper all ready, which many of us speedily consumed . . . and drank some very good wine also," one wrote. After their dinner, they set fire to the building. The British also burned the Capitol, the Treasury, and the navy yard, including all the ships anchored there. The British left within days. Madison and his cabinet returned not long after.

The British set Washington, D.C., ablaze on the night of August 24, 1814.

American spirits were at their lowest. The number of people against the war increased. The government was going broke. The British blockade took a toll on trade. Meanwhile, the British troops marched on to Baltimore, Maryland, but in this city, forces were ready for the British. About one thousand troops stationed in Fort McHenry guarded the entrance

Early on the morning of September 14, 1814, Francis Scott Key points toward the American flag waving over Fort McHenry. Key was thrilled to see the flag because it signaled that the British attack had failed.

The Star Spangled Banner is sung to the tune of "Anacreon in Heaven," a popular British drinking song.

to Baltimore Harbor. The British fleet had to get past the fort to attack the U.S. defensive lines. So on September 13, 1814, the British fired more than 1,500 rounds of ammunition at the fort, hoping it would surrender.

An American named Francis Scott Key was watching the attack from the deck of a British ship. He had come on board to negotiate, or bring about through a discussion, the release of an American prisoner. Once the attack was underway, he couldn't leave the ship. As the long night of bombing continued, Key wondered if Fort McHenry could hold out. The next morning, "by the dawn's early light," he saw the American flag still waving over the fort. The British attack had failed. The sight inspired Key to write a poem called "The Star-Spangled Banner." It was later set to music and became the national anthem.

The British failure at Baltimore ended their invasion in the Chesapeake Bay area. They retreated to the Atlantic Coast. Also in September, U.S. forces turned back another invasion on the Canadian border. An American fleet under Captain Thomas Macdonough beat a British fleet on Lake Champlain. That victory on water forced the British ground invasion to halt and turn back toward Canada. It also convinced British officials in London to look for ways to end the war. Just as the United States was unable to successfully invade Canada, Britain was having trouble making progress in the United States.

Jean Lafitte

The final British invasion was aimed at New Orleans, Louisiana. An army of ten thousand British troops gathered in Jamaica, an island near Cuba, to prepare for the invasion. Many had fought in battles against France. They were considered among Britain's best troops. Racing to meet them and defend New Orleans was Andrew Jackson. Jackson's troops were a ragtag mix of U.S. soldiers and state militia. With the promise of a pardon, or an excuse from punishment, he even enlisted the service of Gulf Coast pirates under Jean Lafitte. The pirates proved to

24

be valuable allies. They knew the region well, and they were outstanding gunmen.

By the end of December, Jackson had formed a defensive line about 1 mile (1.6 km) long, just south of New Orleans. It was defended by about 4,700 troops. When the British began to attack Jackson's line on January 8, 1815, they were hidden in fog. Suddenly, the fog lifted, exposing them to the Americans. Cannons and rifles discharged an intense fire. One British soldier called it "the most murderous I ever beheld."

Volunteers, pirates, and experienced soldiers banded together under the leadership of Andrew Jackson to win the Battle of New Orleans.

Some British troops reached the American lines but were turned back. Others simply fled for cover or hit the ground and remained there until the end of the battle. The British commander, General Sir Edward Pakenham, was killed by a cannonball. Within an hour, the battle was over. The British lost more than two thousand men. The underdogs, the Americans, lost just seventy. It was the most lopsided victory of the war. New Orleans would not be threatened again.

After the Battle of New Orleans, Andrew Jackson was so admired that songs were written in his honor. This photograph shows the sheet music cover from a song celebrating Jackson's victory over the British.

The Battle of New Orleans, the last battle of the War of 1812, actually took place after the two nations had agreed to a peace treaty. British and U.S. representatives had agreed to end the war on December 24, 1814—fifteen days before the British assault on New Orleans. Just as at the beginning of the war, news of the treaty didn't reach North America until it was too late.

Officials on both sides of the Atlantic had become eager to end the war by 1814. The British blockade hurt shopkeepers and farmers. American trade suffered, and the government was unable to raise enough money to fight the war. In New England, members of the Federalist

Party had been against the war from the beginning. In December 1814, they met in Hartford, Connecticut, to express their concerns. The Hartford Convention recommended giving the states—rather than the federal government— more power over defense matters.

Great Britain was discouraged by the U.S. victory on Lake Champlain and the failure of the invasion along the U.S.– Canadian border. Also, the British taxes that paid for war in the United States were becoming more and more unpopular in Great Britain. Peace negotiations began in present-day Ghent, Belgium, in August 1814. The British had a long list of conditions. They wanted control over part of Maine and part of present-day Minnesota. They demanded that the United States remove all warships from the Great Lakes. And they proposed a permanent reservation in the Great Lakes region for their American Indian allies. But as their invasions of the United States failed, they dropped each of these demands.

During a blockade, British warships patrol the Chesapeake Bay to prevent Americans from getting needed supplies.

After signing the Treaty of Ghent, John Quincy Adams (center right) shakes hands with Admiral Lord James Gambier (center left). Adams negotiated the peace treaty with the British, and he later became president of the United States.

The Treaty of Ghent mentioned none of these conditions. Nor did it address the issues that caused the war—free trade or the impressment of sailors. The treaty simply said that these issues would be handled as they were before the war began.

Every member of the U.S. Senate approved the treaty. The war had lasted a little more than two and a half years. More than two thousand Americans died, and more than four thousand were wounded. The United States had been unable to conquer Canada. The peace treaty didn't give Americans any of the rights at sea that they had fought for, but the War of 1812 did have lasting consequences for the nation. Victories in the South resulted in the United States getting Florida from Spain. With the death of Tecumseh, the American Indian threat in the Northwest and South was broken. Tribes were forced to move to lands on the other side of the Mississippi River.

The war also earned the United States more respect overseas. The nation's troops had again stood up to British forces. In fact, Britain never again tried to impress U.S. sailors or restrict trade. Many Americans considered the War of 1812 a "second war of independence." After the War of 1812, the United States was left alone to shape its future—free of the influence of Great Britain.

Evening Gazette Office,
Boston, Monday, 10, A.M.

The following most highly important handbill has just been issued from the Centinel press. We deem it a duty that we owe our Friends and the Public to assist in the prompt spread of the Glorious News.

Treaty of PEACE signed and arrived.

Centinel Office, Feb. 15, 1815, 8 o'clock in the morning.

WE have this instant received in Thirty-two hours from New-York the following

Great and Happy News!
FOR THE PUBLIC.

To BENJAMIN RUSSELL, Esq. Centinel-Office, Boston.
New-York, Feb. 11, 1815—Saturday Evening, 10 o'clock.

SIR—

I HASTEN to acquaint you, for the information of the Public, of the arrival here this afternoon of H. Br. M. sloop of war Favorite, in which has come passenger Mr Carroll, American Messenger, having in his possession

A Treaty of Peace

Between this Country and Great-Britain, signed on the 26th December last.

Mr Baker also is on board, as Agent for the British Government, the same who was formerly Charge des Affairs here.

Mr Carroll reached town at eight o'clock this evening. He shewed to a friend of mine, who is acquainted with him, the packet containing the Treaty, and a London newspaper of the last date of December, announcing the signing of the Treaty

It depends, however, as my friend observed, upon the act of the President to suspend hostilities on this side.

The gentleman left London the 2d Jan. The Transit had sailed previously from a port on the Continent.

This city is in a perfect uproar of joy, shouts, illuminations, &c. &c.

I have undertaken to send you this by Express—the rider engaging to deliver it by Eight o'clock on Monday morning. The expense will be 225 dollars :—If you can collect so much to indemnify me I will thank you to do so.

I am with respect, Sir, your obedient servant,
JONATHAN GOODHUE.

We most gratefully felicitate our Country on this auspicious news, which may be relied on as wholly authentic—CENTINEL.

PEACE EXTRA.

A Boston newspaper put out a special edition to tell people the "Great and Happy News"— the War of 1812 was finally over.

GLOSSARY

ally; plural, allies – a group or country that has joined with another group or country for a special purpose

British warships blockade the Chesapeake Bay.

blockade – (noun) an action by troops or warships to prevent people or supplies from getting to a nation at war or an enemy area; (verb) to close off a harbor or coastline to prevent entrance or exit

commerce – the buying and selling of goods, or trade

Congress – the United States Senate and the House of Representatives

cross fire – lines of fire from two or more positions, crossing one another

deserter – someone who abandons a naval or military post without permission

fortification – a structure, such as a wall or moat, that strengthens or defends

frigate – a small warship, built for speed

frontier – the farthermost area of a settled or developed territory

goods – items that can be bought and sold

hull – the frame or body of a ship

impress – to force into naval service

British ships sometimes stopped U.S. ships and impressed seamen into service in the British Royal Navy.

mast – an upright pole that supports the sails and rigging of a ship or boat

militia – a group trained for emergency military service

reparation – action or payment to make up for a wrong or injury

reservation – a tract of land set aside for a special purpose

trade – the business of buying and selling goods, or commerce

TIMELINE

Revolutionary War with **1783**
Great Britain ends

1807 *June 22: Chesapeake–Leopard* affair

1811 *November 7:* Harrison defeats
Tenskwatawa in Battle of Tippecanoe

1812

June 18: President
Madison signs
declaration of war

1813

April 27: Pike
takes York

August 19: USS
Constitution
defeats HMS
Guerriere

March 27–28:
Jackson defeats
Creeks in Battle of
Horseshoe Bend

1814

September 10:
Perry wins Battle
of Lake Erie

*December 29:*USS
Constitution
defeats HMS *Java*

1815

October 5:
Harrison wins
Battle of the
Thames

August 8: Peace
negotiations begin

August 24: British
seize Washington,
D.C., burn White
House, Capitol,
and Treasury

January 8:
Jackson defeats
British at New
Orleans

February 16:
U.S. Senate
and President
Madison approve
Treaty of Ghent

September 11:
Macdonough wins
Battle of Lake
Champlain

September 14:
Key writes "Star-
Spangled Banner"

December 24: U.S.
and Great Britain
sign Treaty of Ghent

INDEX (**Boldface** page numbers indicate illustrations.)

TO COME

American Indians, 7, 8, 10, 17–18, 27, 29. *See also* individual tribe names
Barron, James, 3
Battle of New Orleans, 24–26
Battle of the Thames, 17
Battle of Tippecanoe, 7
British Royal Navy, 4, 8, 12, 14, 25. *See also* Great Britain, victories for
Calhoun, John C., 9
Canada, conflicts at, 10, 11, 14, 15–16, 18, 20
Castlereagh, Lord, 8
Chauncey, Isaac, 15
Chesapeake, 3, 4, 6, 8
Chesapeake Bay, 20, 24, **27**
Clay, Henry, 6, **6,** 7
Congress, U.S., 6, 8–9
Creek Indians, 18
Dacres, James R., 12–13
Dearborn, Henry, 10
Decatur, Stephen, 14
Embargo Act, 6
Federalist Party, 26–27
Fort Dearborn, 10, **10**
Fort Detroit, 10
Fort McHenry, 22–23
Fort Mims, 18
France, Great Britain's conflict with, 4–5, 19

Frenchtown, 11
Great Britain, victories for, 10–11, 18–19, 20–21
Great Lakes, 7, 8, 15, 27
Harrison, William Henry, 7, 14, **15,** 17
Hartford Convention, 27
HMS *Guerriere*, 12–13
HMS *Java*, 14
HMS *Macedonian*, 14
Hull, Isaac, 12
Hull, William, 10
impressment, 4, 7, 9, 28
Jackson, Andrew, 14, **15,** 18, 24–26
Jefferson, Thomas, 4
Key, Francis Scott, **22,** 23
Lafitte, Jean, 24, **24**
Lake Champlain, 11
Lake Erie, battle at, 16, **16**
Leopard, 3, 8
Macdonough, Thomas, 24
Madison, Dolley, 20, **20**
Madison, James, 8, **8,** 9, 10, 20–21
Monroe, James, 20
Navy, U.S., 12–14. *See also* United States, victories for
Niagara, 16
Niagara Falls, 10, 11
"Old Ironsides." *See* USS *Constitution*

Pakenham, Edward, 26
Perry, Oliver H., 16, **16,** 17
Pike, Zebulon, 15, **15**
pirates, 24–25
Potawatomi Indians, 10
Queenston Heights, 11
Red Sticks, 18
Rush, Richard, 20
Shawnee Indians, 7
"Star Spangled Banner, The," 23, **23**
Tecumseh, 7, **7,** 17, 29
Tenskwatawa, 7
trade restrictions, 5, 6, 7, 8–9, 27
Treaty of Fort Jackson, 18
Treaty of Ghent, 28, **28**
United States, victories for, 12–14, 15, 16–17, 18, 20, 22–23, 24–26
USS *Constitution*, 12, 13, **13**
USS *United States*, 14
War Hawks, 6–7, 8, 9
War of 1812
   declaration of war, 9
   opinions about, 9
   opposition to, 11–12
   peace treaty, 26–28
Washington, D.C., battle at, 20–21, **21**
Washington Federalist, 4

PHOTO CREDITS

Photographs ©: Corbis-Bettmann: cover (Francis G. Mayer), 1, 3, 6, 8, 15 top right, 15 top left, 16, 21, 22, 28, 31 top right, 31 left; Liaison Agency, Inc.: 26 (Hulton Getty); North Wind Picture Archives: 7, 13 (N. Carter), 2, 10, 17, 20, 25, 27, 29, 30 top, 31 bottom right; Stock Montage, Inc.: 5, 15 bottom, 19, 24, 30 bottom; The Benecke Rare Book and Manuscript Library Yale University: 23.

Maps by TJS Design, Inc.

PICTURE IDENTIFICATIONS

Cover photo: The USS *Constitution* and the HMS *Guerriere* fought from a distance of about 10 yards (9 m).
Page 1: William Henry Harrison's men and American Indians fought at close range during the Battle of Tippecanoe.
Page 2: American seamen capture a British ship during the War of 1812.

ABOUT THE AUTHOR

Andrew Santella lives in Chicago. He writes for newspapers and magazines, including *The New York Times Book Review* and *GQ*. Mr. Santella is also the author of several other books for Children's Press: *Impeachment*, *The Capitol*, *The Chisholm Trail*, *Illinois*, and *Thomas Jefferson: Voice of Liberty*.